The Story of the Tree
That Came to Life

Written by

Tony Scott

Illustrations by

Theresa Anne Stites

Hi! My name is Leaf.
I have a story you won't believe!

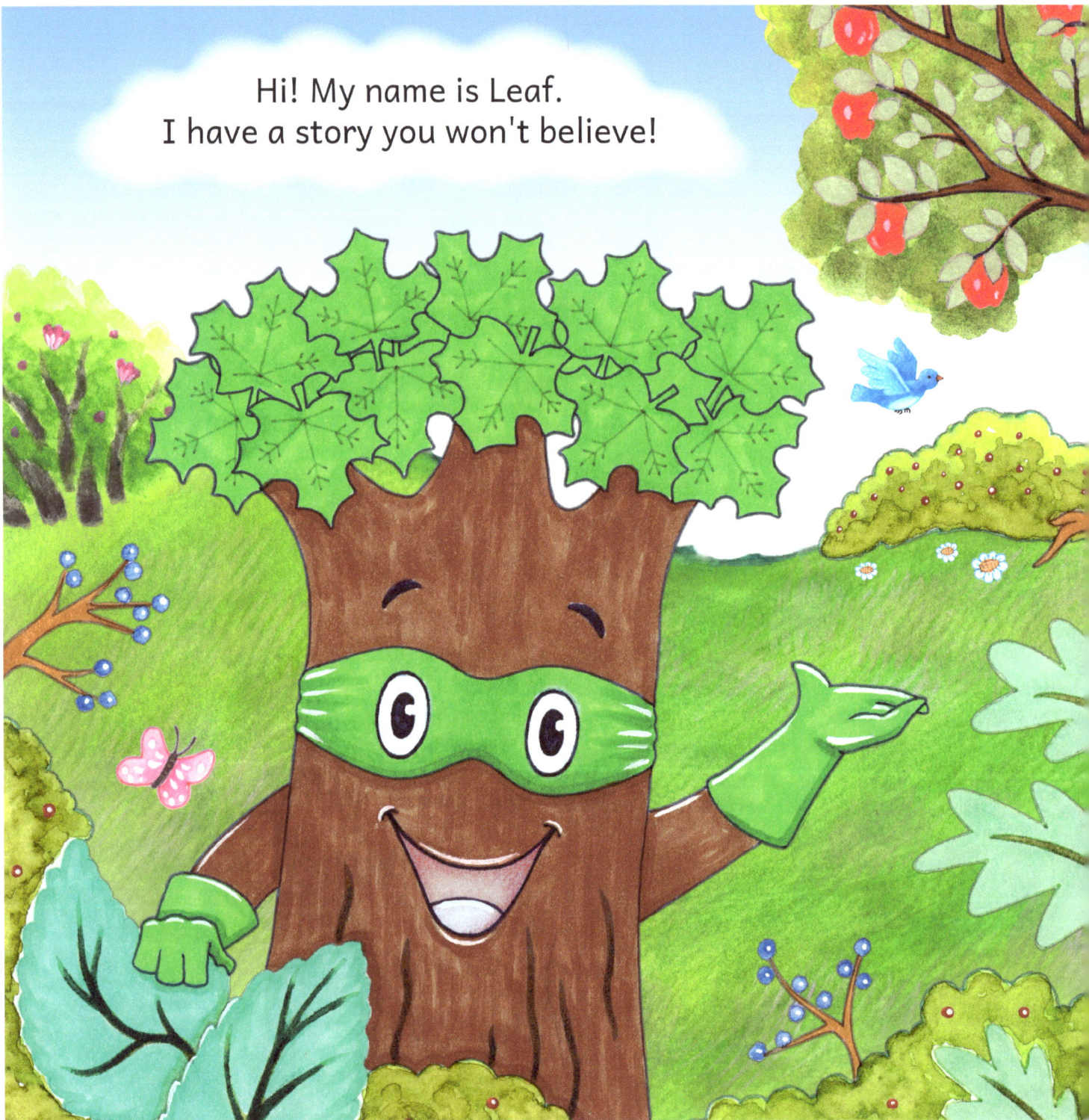

It starts in the Garden with a man named Adam and a woman named Eve.

In the midst of the Garden, two trees God did place, representing your life and your earthly race.

The Tree of Life stands so very tall;
the other tree will cause you in sin to fall.
On each tree, there was fruit so sweet,
but from the Tree of Knowledge of
Good and Evil, you should not eat.

*"But of the Tree of the Knowledge of
Good and Evil and blessing and calamity you
shall not eat, for in the day that you eat of
it you shall surely die."*
Genesis 2:17 AMPC

Each day we live, our life consists of making a choice;
from the Tree of Life, you will hear His voice.
From His Red Letter Teachings, He speaks so clear,
and calls upon us His words to hear.

*"People were bringing little
children to Jesus for Him to
place His hands on them, but
the disciples rebuked them.
When Jesus saw this, He was
indignant. He said to them,
'Let the little children come to
me, and do not hinder them,
for the Kingdom of God belongs
to such as these. Truly I tell you,
anyone who will not receive
the Kingdom of God like a little
child will never enter it.'
And He took the children in His
arms, placed His hands on
them and blessed them."*
Mark 10:13-16

In the Bible, the trees often appear.
The lesson they teach, you surely must hear.

In the Tree of Life, secure you will forever be.
From the Tree of Knowledge of Good and Evil,
you must flee.

As it was in the beginning, in the beautiful Garden, this Tree will come again offering a great pardon.

From the time of Adam and Eve, until our own day, God's plan for the Tree was to offer us a new way.

Jesus came from Heaven in the Father's love.
The Holy Spirit was upon Him like a peaceful dove.

To forgive our sins is the reason He came,
to take away our guilt and all of our shame.

All of us have sinned and are in need of a Savior;
His wonderful love transforms our behavior.

The Tree of Life becomes for us a Cross,
where Jesus redeems all that we have lost.

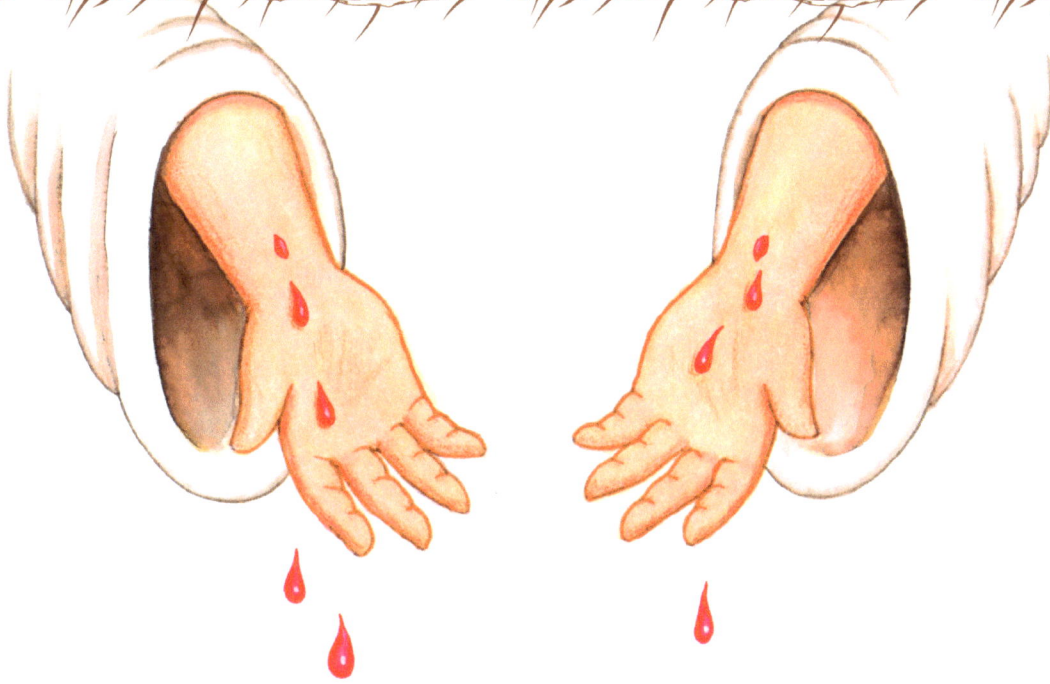

His blood poured out, from my sins, I am free-
all because He was willing to die upon that Tree.
By the sacrifice of His life, He saved my soul.
His Death and Resurrection broke Satan's control.

As a worshiping angel in Heaven, Satan was known–
a beautiful musician singing around God's Throne.

Then he rebelled and from Heaven was cast.
He lives on Earth to remind us of our past.

"Thank you, Father!"

When Jesus rose up from the grave,
the road to Heaven our Savior did pave.

Today, Jesus sits at the Father's right hand,
so you and I can live the life for us He planned.

THE ROMAN ROAD

Romans 3:23
"For all have sinned, and come short of the glory of God."

Romans 6:23
"The wages of sin is death; but the gift of God is eternal life through Jesus Christ our Lord."

Romans 5:8
"But God demonstrates His own love toward us, in that, while we were yet sinners, Christ died for us."

Romans 10:9
"That if you confess with your mouth, 'Jesus is Lord,' and believe in your heart that God raised Him from the dead, you will be saved."

Each day we live, a choice we must make.
And on that choice, so much is at stake.
Satan tempts us to sin, God's Word disobey,
but when we do, a price we must pay.

The Tree of Life in the Garden was Jesus indeed.
By His death on the Cross-Tree, from sin, we were freed.

He knew as His children, we would often come short.
With the Tree of Life, we always have His support.
He gives us every reason, His Name to praise.
Jesus is our Tree of Life to live all our days.

"Thank you, Jesus!"

"Welcome, My Child."

When this life is over, and in Heaven we arrive,
forever with Him, we will eternally thrive.

The Tree of Life again we will see,
and in His Presence, always we'll be.

Coming from the Throne, a crystal clear river is flowing.
On each side, the Tree of Life is growing.

From the Garden of Eden to the Cross-Tree,
where He died, and now in Heaven, we do abide.

The Scriptures we read tell us of His-story.
Throughout the Bible, the Tree of Life reveals His Glory.

Eat from the Tree of Life, and from it never depart.
Stay close to Jesus, and let Him fill your heart.

Become a Tree of Life, allowing others to know.
Always to your friends, His love you must show.
From the Tree of Life, I became.
And, like me, you can do the very same.

You can make Jesus your
forever friend-
living the life for you,
He did intend.

Read your Bible,
and say your prayers.
Give your heart to Jesus-
He always cares.

The Day the Tree Came Alive in Me

I, _____ ,
accept Jesus Christ as my
Lord and Savior.

Date _____

About the Author
Tony Scott

He is a nationally and internationally recognized teacher, dedicated writer, and visionary leader. Though he spends much of his time in front of his congregation at theChurch Maumee, where he has pastored for over 50 years, he enjoys writing poems, study materials, sermons, and books. His heart for God and his pursuit of Him brought a depth of content concerning how God's Kingdom operates into our current world. He feels the world is in dire need of hearing His Truth from the Word, the realness of the Kingdom, and how to live out your highest life.

About theChurch & theTree

At theChurch, it's not about religion but discovering the real. Our mission is to reach people for God, both locally and globally, teach people the transformational way of Jesus, train people to impact every arena of their life, and release people to fulfill their God-given destiny. We pray that His Word will commit us to pursue total transformation—spirit, soul, body.

www.ingramcontent.com/pod-product-compliance
Lightning Source LLC
Chambersburg PA
CBHW041556040426

42447CB00002B/190